YESTERDAY'S STRENGTH, TOMORROW'S WEAKNESS

How to Evolve Infrastructure to Stay Ahead of Climate Challenges

YESTERDAY'S STRENGTH, TOMORROW'S WEAKNESS

How to Evolve Infrastructure to Stay Ahead of Climate Challenges

Prashant Kabra

Available on amazonkindle

Worldwide Published by

Pendown Press
PREMIUM BUSINESS PUBLISHER

PENDOWN PRESS LLP

An ISO 9001 & ISO 14001 Certified Co.,

Regd. Office: 3767A, Kanhaiya Nagar,

Tri Nagar, Delhi-110035

Ph.: 8130886000, 9650072927

E-mail: info@pendownpress.com

Branch Office: 1A/2A, 20, Hari Sadan, Ansari Road,

Daryaganj, New Delhi-110002

Ph.: 011-45794768

Website: PendownPress.com

Edition: 2025

Price: ₹299

ISBN: 978-93-6338-509-2

Layout and Cover Designed by Pendown Graphics Team

Printed and Bound in India by Thomson Press India Ltd.

Contents

Two Bonus Chapters on Strategic Monitoring and Cutting-Edge Safety Enhancements

Preface

Infrastructure: The Foundation For The Future

Infrastructure is the backbone of progress —

Whether it's roads, bridges, power plants, or buildings, every project starts with a vision for the future.

However, as we all know, the path from vision to reality is fraught with challenges—some that we can foresee and others that we can't.

I've spent decades working in the field of geotechnical engineering and infrastructure development.

Throughout this journey, I've learned that success comes down to one thing—**Preparation.**

The world is changing rapidly, and the old ways of doing things simply aren't enough anymore. Today, we need solutions that can not only meet current demands but are built to withstand the challenges of tomorrow.

This book is designed for project heads, engineers, and decision-makers who are at the forefront of building tomorrow's world.

It brings together decades of insights, innovations, and

lessons from countless projects across India and beyond.

Through real-world examples, advanced frameworks, and practical tools, this book will give you the edge to complete your projects on time, within budget, and with confidence that they will stand the test of time.

Whether you're just getting started or you're an industry veteran looking for fresh perspectives, this book will serve as a valuable guide on your journey.

The infrastructure world is evolving, and it's time we evolve with it.

Let's build the future together.

Acknowledgements

As a rule, we consider a debt to be bad, but there is a good debt too.

I take pride in carrying a good one always- the debt of gratitude towardMy life, my wife & two sons, along with my team and friends, forever as an extended family.

My mentor and Guru, Akshar Yadav, who transformed me to the level of being born again, with love for my life and happiness in business as my true gains.

My past & present team members, who have been strong pillars of support.

And my customers as my true companions.

A special acknowledgement goes to Dinesh Verma and his wonderful team at Pendown Press. From the initial concept to the final manuscript, their support and expertise have made this book possible.

Chapter

01

The Why Behind This Book

In the ever-changing world of infrastructure and advanced geotechnical engineering, you need to keep up with new ideas and changes to stay on top.

Particularly, project heads and senior engineers leading or working on high-stake projects that hold human and material assets and projects that need health monitoring and predictability.

The primary objective of this book is *to share valuable insights and useful actionable tips with project leaders and engineers.* The focus is on imparting cutting-edge geotechnical solutions that can transform how they tackle infrastructure projects.

This book is unique because it integrates the traditional wisdom of old-school engineering methods with new technological breakthroughs. It brings together the latest ideas in live tracking, number crunching, and advanced technologies, equipping readers with a blueprint to navigate the toughest challenges in infrastructure projects.

Here's what this book will empower you with:

- **A Comprehensive Understanding:** A deep dive into the critical aspects of geotechnical solutions, from predictive maintenance to climate resilience.
- **Practical Tools:** Actionable steps and practical tools that can be immediately implemented to enhance project outcomes.
- **Real-World Applications:** Case studies and success stories that demonstrate the effectiveness of the discussed solutions.
- **Strategic Insights:** In-depth analysis of the IAS 5.0 Framework, offering a holistic approach to infrastructure integrity and sustainability.

By the end of this book, geotechnical project heads and teams as well as infra-project stakeholders will be equipped with the knowledge and tools needed to transform their infrastructure projects, ensuring they are not only efficient and cost-effective but also resilient and future-proof.

Chapter

02

Who Am I?

I am a passionate geotechnical and infrastructure specialist, with over three decades of experience.

My journey into the world of geosciences and infrastructure began in the early 1990s, driven by my deep love for earth sciences and technological innovation. Over the years, I have found myself engaged in solving complex geotechnical challenges through cutting-edge solutions.

With a unique approach to solving problems at their root, rather than just addressing symptoms, I have worked on over 1200 projects and helped more than 400 clients globally, transforming their infrastructure landscapes with my out-of-the-box strategies.

My journey has been one of constant learning and innovation.

From my early days in college, I realized that traditional methods of addressing infrastructure problems were time-consuming and ineffective. This led me to explore new technologies and methods that could revolutionize the field.

After years of observation, analysis, and hands-on practice, I developed several innovative frameworks and tools, including

the IAS 5.0 Framework, and S M A R T Framework that have transformed how we approach infrastructure health monitoring, predictive maintenance, and disaster mitigation.

These efforts culminated in the creation of this book, which serves as a guide for project leaders and engineers to leverage advanced geotechnical solutions to solve modern infrastructure challenges.

I express my heartfelt gratitude to my dedicated team, clients, government bodies, and private players I have had the privilege of working with. Their unwavering trust and collaboration have been instrumental in shaping the success of my career and the solutions I have developed.

Their confidence in me has made 'Prashant Kabra'- an Infrascientist- a trusted name in the infrastructure and geotechnical engineering field.

Chapter

03

The Journey of Innovation – What Makes Me So Confident in Transforming Your Infrastructure Projects

I'm **Prashant Kabra #India's Top Expert in Solving Infra-Geo Challenges.** I am here to bring new, tech-based answers to old Infra and Geo problems., To date, I have completed 1200 projects and helped over 400 clients achieve geo-scientific efficiency and success in their infra projects.

It all began in the early 1990s.

My love for earth sciences and technologies grew during my college days.

I noticed that the old ways of fixing infrastructure issues were taking too long and often missing the real problems.

This made me look for new innovative technologies and methods to change the field.

How it started!

When I started my career and encountered challenges, I viewed them not merely as things to be fixed but as problems that needed to be addressed so that they never occurred again.

I therefore started to work on the root cause of the problems and not just on the symptoms.

The focus of my study was how soil works and how it affects buildings!

Gradually, my hard work and new ideas caught the eye of big names in the industry.

I started working with the government and private companies bringing advanced ground engineering solutions to many projects.

One of my first big wins was in protecting and steadying slopes. By mixing new synthetic materials with old engineering ways, I created solutions that worked better and lasted longer.

This new approach paved the way for many more advances to come.

Game-Changing Innovations

The Revolutionary IAS 5.0 Framework

My constant drive for the best results led to the creation of the IAS 5.0 Framework, an all-terrain system to fix all infrastructure problems and gaps. This system combines cutting-edge tracking tools, powerful data analysis, and instant insights to give a complete picture of infrastructure projects. This perfect diagnosis is then executed with the application of the right product solution to achieve desirable results.

This is what the industry had wanted for years! They responded with joy, testimonials, awards, and appreciation......

1. "Initially, we were concerned about the durability and effectiveness of the pond lining.

However, Sanbros Spares Pvt Ltd exceeded our expectations. Their team was professional, used top-notch materials, and ensured a leak-proof installation. Now, we have peace of mind knowing the pond is secure and reliable. The process was smooth, and the results are outstanding. Highly recommend!"

– Mr. S.K. Tiwari, Dec 2024
Railways Engineering Dept.

---

2. "We had some doubts about the long-term effectiveness of slope protection for our project, but Sanbros Spares Pvt Ltd proved us wrong. The team not only met our expectations but went above and beyond. The work was completed on time with premium materials, and the protection is strong and reliable, preventing any erosion. We can confidently say they've added significant value to our operations. Highly recommended!"

– Mr. Janardhan Nadkarni, March 2024
Chief Manager Head, Civil Hydro

---

3. "We were looking for a precise and timely solution, and Sanbros Spares Pvt Ltd delivered exactly that. They addressed all our concerns about quality and timing, ensuring the project was executed flawlessly. Professional, efficient, and on schedule – a great choice for any project."

– Mr. A. Vishwakarma, Nov 2020

Rail SECR Dy CE GN

---

4. "We were initially uncertain about finding a reliable team for our drain line work, but Sanbros Spares Pvt Ltd made the process effortless. Their professional approach, efficient execution, and high-quality results delivered on time ensured we were fully satisfied with the project. We had no issues, and the project was completed successfully as promised."

– Mr. Kohali, Feb 2024

Sr. Section Engineer

---

5. "We had concerns about the construction process of the haul road, but Sanbros Spares Pvt Ltd handled everything smoothly. The process was transparent, the work was exceptional, and it has proven to be a valuable asset to our operations. We now have a durable, efficient road that makes a significant difference in our daily functions."

– Mr. Sanjay Singh, Dec 2024

SO Civil, MCL

6. "We were cautious about whether the slope protection would truly prevent erosion long-term. Sanbros Spares Pvt Ltd has exceeded our expectations. The work was highly effective in safeguarding our property, and the results are visible immediately. It's a lasting solution that gives us confidence in the integrity of our site."

– Mr. Ajeet Kumar, Jan 2025

Chapter

04

Understanding Market Realities

The infrastructure and geotechnical sectors are tensed with challenges that often stem from deep-rooted misconceptions and outdated practices. To effectively address these challenges, it is crucial to first understand the current market realities and the common issues faced by project heads and engineers.

A. Myths and Misconceptions

1. Myth: Conventional Methods Are Good Enough To Get The Job Done

Reality: Today's infrastructure projects are becoming more complex, and with climate change playing a bigger role, there's a growing need for solutions that are not just advanced but also adaptable.

2. Myth: One-Size-Fits-All Solutions

Reality: Infrastructure projects are unique, each presenting its own set of challenges. Generic solutions often fall short, and what's really needed are approaches tailored to the specific demands of each project.

3. **Myth: Cutting-Edge Technologies Are Very Expensive**

Reality: While it's true that the upfront costs of advanced technologies like DFOS and Qmax might seem steep, however, these innovations pay off eventually by cutting down on maintenance expenses and extending the life of the infrastructure with the least botheration.

B. Situational Challenges & Solutions

The market struggles with situational challenges too. These challenges are primarily the result of a typical mindset of responding in less brilliant way.

1. **Reacting to Disasters vs. Proactive Planning**

Many projects tend to react only when a problem pops up instead of planning ahead for potential issues. This reactive stance can end up costing more and increasing risks.

2. **Striking a Balance Between Cost and Quality**

There's a common tendency in the market to opt for cheaper, short-term fixes over more durable, long-lasting solutions. However, this can put the safety and longevity of infrastructure projects at risk.

3. **Navigating Regulatory Hurdles**

Keeping up with ever-changing regulations is no small feat. Streamlining this process is key to ensuring projects get executed smoothly and efficiently.

Chapter

05

What's the Solution?

Infrastructure projects often face unique geotechnical challenges that require tailored solutions. A one-size-fits-all approach is rarely effective in addressing the specific issues of different sites.

One must understand the importance of developing custom solutions for geotechnical challenges for effective results and installing legacy projects.

The Need for Custom Solutions

Every infrastructure project is unique, with its own set of geotechnical conditions and challenges. Custom solutions are essential because they:

1. **Address Specific Site Conditions:** Tailored solutions consider the unique soil properties, topography, and environmental conditions of each site.
2. **Enhance Effectiveness:** Custom solutions are designed to target the root causes of geotechnical issues, ensuring more effective and long-lasting results.

3. **Optimize Costs:** By focusing on specific needs, custom solutions can reduce unnecessary expenses and optimize resource use.
4. **Improve Safety:** Addressing site-specific risks enhances the overall safety of the infrastructure project.

How to make it work

Since the most effective scientific approach to address geotechnical issues lies in customized solutions, we have devised a framework- the **IAS 5.0 Framework**- equipped to solve all geo-infra challenges with accuracy and durability.

This framework is the result of over two decades of hands-on practical site interventions to achieve targeted goals.

This IAS 5.0 Framework covers all geo-infra challenges broadly into five major segments.

1. **Urban Development & Architectural Stability (UDAS):** Deals with tall buildings and city planning.
2. **Infrastructure Integrity & Mobility Enhancement (IIME):** Improves roads and city transport systems.
3. **Disaster Mitigation & Infrastructure Resilience (DMIR):** Gets ready for natural disasters and builds tough emergency response structures.
4. **Environmental Conservation & Coastal Protection (ECCP):** Puts in place waste handling answers and stops coastal wearing away.

5. **Resource Management & Renewable Energy Foundations (RMREF):** Ensures mining is done in a long-lasting way and sets up renewable energy projects.

Each segment of the IAS 5.0 Framework is focused on tackling specific problems, offering custom solutions that make infrastructure projects safer, more efficient, and longer-lasting.

Chapter

06

Unlocking IAS 5.0 Framework Functioning

This framework offers a step-wise protocol to gain desired results within scheduled time slabs.

For execution, it starts with:

- Challenge Mapping
- Expert consultation
- Leveraging advanced technologies
- Evaluation of the performance-oriented processes

This helps in creating a result-centric high-performance solution which is potent enough to mitigate the challenge.

Step-wise Solution Development

1. **Comprehensive Site Assessments**
   - Conduct detailed site assessments to understand the unique geotechnical conditions and challenges.
   - Use advanced tools such as soil sampling, geophysical surveys, and remote sensing to gather accurate data.

2. **Collaboration with Experts**
    - Work with geotechnical engineers, environmental scientists, and other experts to develop tailored solutions.
    - Leverage their expertise to design solutions that address the specific needs of the site.
3. **Use of Advanced Technologies**
    - Incorporate advanced technologies such as geosynthetics, DFOS, and predictive modelling to enhance the effectiveness of custom solutions.
    - Example: Using geosynthetic materials for slope stabilization, tailored to the specific soil composition and slope angle of the site.
4. **Iterative Design and Testing**
    - Develop multiple design iterations and conduct tests to evaluate their effectiveness.

Use simulation tools to predict the performance of different solutions under various conditions.

Custom Slope Stabilization Solution: A Case Study

The Concern: A project involving a slope prone to erosion and landslides.

The Preliminary Assessment: A comprehensive site assessment reveals that the soil is highly prone to erosion due to its high water runoff, sandy composition, and steep gradient.

The Solution Process: To address this challenge, a custom solution is developed in the following steps-

1. **Assessment:** Detailed soil analysis and topographical surveys identify the specific areas at risk.
2. **Design:** A combination of geosynthetic materials and vegetation is used to stabilize the slope. Geosynthetic liners prevent soil erosion, while deep-rooted plants provide additional stability.
3. **Implementation:** The solution is implemented in stages, with continuous monitoring to assess its effectiveness.
4. **Evaluation:** The slope is monitored using DFOS technology to ensure that the stabilization measures are working as intended.

This custom solution addresses the unique challenges of the site, providing a durable and effective method for slope stabilization.

Integrating Custom Solutions with the IAS 5.0 Framework

The IAS 5.0 Framework supports the development and implementation of custom geotechnical solutions:

1. **Data Integration:** The framework integrates data from site assessments and monitoring tools to inform the design of custom solutions.

2. **Real-Time Monitoring:** Continuous monitoring ensures that the custom solutions are effective and allows for adjustments as needed.
3. **Holistic Approach:** The framework combines advanced technologies and expert insights to develop comprehensive solutions tailored to the specific needs of each project.

Actionable Steps for Implementing Custom Geotechnical Solutions

To develop and implement custom geotechnical solutions effectively, follow these steps:

- **Conduct Detailed Site Assessments:** Use advanced tools to gather accurate data on the geotechnical conditions of the site.
- **Collaborate with Experts:** Engage with geotechnical engineers and other experts to develop tailored solutions.
- **Design and Test Solutions:** Create multiple design iterations and test their effectiveness using simulation tools.
- **Implement and Monitor:** Implement the custom solutions in stages and use real-time monitoring to assess their performance.
- **Adjust as Needed:** Continuously evaluate the effectiveness of the solutions and adjust as necessary.

By adopting a tailored approach to geotechnical challenges, you can ensure that your infrastructure projects are safe, effective, and sustainable.

Chapter

07

Infrastructure Health Monitoring and Predictive Maintenance

Maintaining the health and integrity of infrastructure projects is a critical aspect of ensuring their long-term functionality and safety.

However, traditional maintenance methods, which often rely on reactive measures, can lead to costly repairs and unexpected downtimes.

The IAS 5.0 Framework incorporates health monitoring and predictive maintenance as key components of its comprehensive approach to infrastructure management:

1. **Continuous Monitoring:** The framework uses advanced technologies like DFOS and IoT sensors to provide real-time data on infrastructure conditions.
2. **Predictive Analytics:** Advanced data analytics tools process the collected data, identifying patterns and predicting maintenance needs.

3. **Proactive Interventions:** The framework enables proactive maintenance activities, ensuring infrastructure remains in optimal condition.

Why Health Monitoring and Predictive Maintenance?

1. **Early Detection of Issues:** Continuous monitoring allows for the early identification of potential problems, preventing minor issues from escalating into major failures.
2. **Enhanced Safety:** Regular health checks ensure that infrastructure remains safe for use, protecting both workers and the public.
3. **Cost Efficiency:** Predictive maintenance reduces the need for expensive emergency repairs and extends the lifespan of infrastructure assets.
4. **Operational Continuity:** By minimizing unexpected downtimes, predictive maintenance ensures that infrastructure remains operational and efficient.

Predictive Maintenance Techniques

1. **Data Analytics:** Advanced data analytics can process the vast amounts of data collected by monitoring technologies, and identify patterns and trends that indicate potential issues.
   - **Example:** Machine learning algorithms can analyse historical data from DFOS sensors to predict when and where maintenance will be needed.

2. **Condition-Based Maintenance (CBM):** CBM involves performing maintenance activities based on the actual condition of the infrastructure rather than on a fixed schedule.

   - **Example:** Regularly updated sensor data can trigger maintenance activities only when certain thresholds are reached, ensuring timely and necessary interventions.

3. **Digital Twins:** A digital twin is a virtual replica of a physical infrastructure asset that can be used to simulate and predict the effects of various conditions and scenarios.

   - **Example:** A digital twin of a railway bridge can simulate the impact of heavy loads and extreme weather, helping engineers plan maintenance activities accordingly.

Predictive Maintenance in Tunnel Management: A Use Case Scenario

The effective application of predictive maintenance in managing railway tunnels.

- By deploying DFOS and IoT sensors throughout the tunnels, continuous data on structural integrity, temperature, and vibrations can be collected.
- This data is then analysed using advanced analytics to identify early signs of wear and potential issues.

- As a result, maintenance activities can be scheduled proactively, preventing disruptions and ensuring the tunnels remain safe and operational.

Advanced Technologies for Health Monitoring

1. **Distributed Fiber Optic Sensing (DFOS)**

   DFOS technology uses fibre optic cables as continuous sensors to monitor various parameters such as strain, temperature, and vibrations. This provides real-time insights into the health of infrastructure.

2. **Remote Sensing and Drones**

   Drones equipped with high-resolution cameras and sensors can perform aerial inspections, capturing detailed images and data of hard-to-reach areas.

Internet of Things (IoT) Sensors

IoT sensors can be embedded in infrastructure to continuously collect data on various parameters such as temperature, humidity, and pressure.

Integrating Health Monitoring with the IAS 5.0 Framework with Actionable Steps

To effectively implement health monitoring and predictive maintenance in your infrastructure projects, consider the following steps:

- **Identify Critical Assets:** Determine which infrastructure assets are critical to your operations and require continuous monitoring.
- **Select Appropriate Technologies:** Choose monitoring technologies such as DFOS, drones, and IoT sensors that best suit your needs.
- **Integrate Data Analytics:** Implement data analytics tools to process the collected data and provide actionable insights.
- **Develop a Maintenance Plan:** Create a predictive maintenance plan based on the insights from data analytics, ensuring timely interventions.
- **Train Your Team:** Provide training for your team on how to use the monitoring technologies and interpret the data effectively.

By adopting advanced health monitoring and predictive maintenance techniques, you can enhance the safety, efficiency, and longevity of your infrastructure projects.

Chapter

08

It's Time to Change!

In the sphere of infrastructural construction especially across different terrains and segments, conventional techniques are considered as the pillars of geo and infrastructural issues.

Undoubtedly, these methods are used frequently in organizations, and mostly as workaround solutions but with changes in the dynamics of the infrastructure and environmental canvas, it's time to work out efficient and advanced solutions that offer a future-proof status to infrastructure.

So, it's better to analyze existing conventional approaches, assess their effectiveness, and explore better contemporary approaches for greater efficiency, less headaches, and better flexibility.

A Compatibility Review of Conventional Geo-Infra Methods

A. For Slope Protection

- **Stone Pitching:** Although the method can be aesthetically pleasing, problems such as flexibility, drainage, and maintenance bring high costs and low possibilities of soil reinforcement.

- **Shotcrete:** Shotcrete is well known for applications where fast construction is required, but it has some drawbacks such as – low ductility or a poor ability to accommodate movement of slopes, brittleness, cracking, and therefore long-term stability may be an issue.
- **Gabions:** These are prone to rusting and require frequent maintenance. Their performance is worse over large and active slopes; hence they are a cause of worry when it comes to environmental conservation.
- **Coir Mats and Retaining Walls:** These options lack a lot of durability and flexibility as compared to the above-mentioned techniques. Also, if walls are not constructed carefully, they may undergo structural failures and cause problems in the drainage system.

B. For Drainage Solutions

- **Stone Masonry and Concrete Forms (PCC and RCC):** These traditional forms of discharge systems are rigid, require labour input, and are not so efficient hydraulically, making them prone to constant maintenance issues and erosion.
- **Bituminous and Vegetative Linings:** These are solutions that ensure momentarily problems get

rectified and act as a one-time solution that is environmentally demanding in nature. The vegetative solutions demand high maintenance and prove to be ineffective in high-risk areas.

C. **For Road Construction**

- **Stabilization Methods (Lime, Cement, Bituminous, and Fly Ash):** Each one is not without its own set of problems including environmental effects, costs, and ineffectiveness on various types of soils and their moisture content.

D. **For Waterproofing**

- **From Lime Mortar to Rubberized Membranes: The** methods vary from having low water resistance and high vulnerability to environmental impacts to having problems in installation and repair.

Modern Effective Solutions

Acknowledging the gaps in conventional methods, here are cutting-edge alternatives that enhance both functionality and economic viability.

A. **For Slope Protection**

- **3 D Confinement Protector, CRGR Nets, and GCCM Technologies:** Compared with conventional methods, these solutions provide greater flexibility, durability, and resistance to environmental damage as well as the need for repair and maintenance.

B. **For Drainage Solutions**

- **Advanced GCCM Technologies:** These are state-of-the-art materials that aim to provide the best solutions for drainage systems that are flexible, economical, and less invasive to the ecology.

C. **For Road Construction**

- **Combinations like PP BIAXIAL SEPARATOR + NON-WOVEN and WOVEN Geotextiles:** These composites provide greater strength, long life, and better protection from environment and forces, thereby providing the desired performance from road structures.

D. **For Waterproofing**

- **Innovative GCCM Options:** Easy to install, fairly flexible, and rather durable materials that address the challenges with efficiency.

In fact, current-day infrastructure development needs to move to more innovative, robust, and less expensive approaches.

Through the implementation of these progressive options, the project heads in the government, public sectors, and private playfield can avoid the construction of structures that may fail within a short period due to changes in the environmental conditions and in return, get robust structures that would be efficient to accommodate the changes for longer durations irrespective of natural geological changes.

Quick Check

Are you still relying on any of the following traditional methods to address Geo/Infra Challenges?

Here's a quick chart to check and below it are individual charts detailing the limitations and disadvantages of these traditional methods.

Traditional Geo-Infra Solutions At A Glance			
For Slope	**For Drains**	**For Roads**	**For Waterproofing**
Stone Pitching	Stone Masonry	Lime Stabilization	Lime Mortar and Plaster
Shotcrete	PCC	Bituminous Stabilization	Bitumen or Tar Mats
High Tensile Steel Cubes (HTS Cubes)	RCC	Cement Stabilization	Mud and Clay
CoirMats	Bituminous Lining	Fly-Ash Stabilization	Rubberized Waterproof Membranes
Retaining Walls	Vegetative Lining	Mechanical Stabilization	Cement Mortar Coating
Making Benches or Berms	Bamboo Matting	-	-

Traditional solutions act as a band-aid and not a permanent solution.

Here's a chart listing the limitations of these traditional solutions.

For Slope Protection					
Stone Pitching	**Shotcrete**	**Gabions**	**Coir Mats**	**Retaining Walls**	**Making Benches or Berms**
Lack of Flexibility	Brittleness and Cracking	Susceptibility to Corrosion	Limited Durability	Structural Failure Due to Poor Design	Limited Long-Term Effectiveness
Labour-Intensive and Expensive	Poor Adaptation to Slope Movement	High Maintenance Requirements	Weak Structural Support	Inadequate Drainage	Soil Erosion and Sediment Accumulation
Limited Soil Reinforcement	High Cost and Maintenance	Limited Effectiveness in Large-Scale or Active Slopes	Ineffective in High-Risk Areas	High Cost and Complexity	High Maintenance Needs
Insufficient Drainage	Environmental Impact	Aesthetic and Environmental Concerns	Maintenance Requirements	Limited Flexibility	Limited Structural Support

For Drain Lining					
Stone Masonry	**PCC (Plain Cement Concrete)**	**RCC (Reinforced Cement Concrete)**	**Bituminous Lining**	**Vegetative Lining**	**Bamboo Matting**
Lack of Flexibility	Brittleness and Cracking	Corrosion of Reinforcement	Limited Lifespan	Limited Durability	Short Lifespan
Labour-Intensive Construction	Poor Adaptation to Ground Movement	High Initial Cost & Complexity	Susceptibility to Degradation	High Maintenance Requirements	Vulnerability to Decay and Pests
Erosion and Undermining	High Maintenance Requirements	Rigid and Inflexible	High Maintenance and Replacement Costs	Slow Establishment Time	Limited Application in Large-Scale or High-Flow Drains
Limited Hydraulic Efficiency	Limited Durability in Harsh Environments	Vulnerability to Cracking	Environmental Impact	Limited Effectiveness in High-Risk Areas	Weak Structural Support

For Subgrade Stabilization				
Lime Stabilization	**Bituminous Stabilization**	**Cement Stabilization**	**Fly Ash Stabilization**	**Mechanical Stabilization**
Limited Applicability to Certain Soil Types	Brittleness and Cracking	Brittleness and Cracking	Variability in Fly Ash Quality	Limited Long-Term Stability
Environmental Sensitivity	High Cost and Resource Intensive	High Environmental Footprint	Environmental and Health Concerns	High Maintenance Requirements
Slow Reaction Time	Poor Long-Term Durability	Limited Flexibility	Limited Effectiveness on Non-Cohesive Soils	Poor Performance in Wet Conditions
Susceptibility to Moisture Variations	Environmental Impact	Labour-Intensive and Expensive	Dependency on Water Content	Limited Resistance to Environmental Changes

For Basement And Roof Waterproofing				
Lime Mortar and Plaster	**Bitumen or Tar Mats**	**Mud and Clay**	**Rubberized Waterproof Membranes**	**Cement Mortar Coating**
Low Water Resistance	Susceptibility to Temperature Fluctuations	Poor Waterproofing Performance	Vulnerability to Punctures and Tears	Brittleness and Cracking
Prone to Cracking	Short Lifespan.	Vulnerability to Erosion and Deformation	UV Degradation	Low Flexibility
Slow Setting and Curing Time	Difficult Installation	High Maintenance	Shorter Lifespan in Harsh Environments	Limited Water Resistance
Limited Durability	Environmental and Health Concerns	Limited Structural Integrity	Difficult Repairs	High Maintenance

Now that you are well aware of the limitations and challenges of the traditional geo-infra methods, IT IS TIME TO CHANGE and overcome these limitations by using new-age modern solutions that are more effective, efficient, sustaining, and even economical in the long run.

Shared below is a quick reference table that shows you which solution to use where. So, get, set, ready & gooo……

Most Effective Alternative Modern Geo-Infra Solutions At A Glance			
For Slopes (Protection)	**For Drains (Linings)**	**For Roads (Subgrade Stabilization)**	**For Waterproofing (Both Basement & Roof)**
GCCM - 1, 2, 3	GCCM - 1, 2	4 in 1 CRPS	GCCM - 1, 2
GCCM - 4	GCCM - 4	6 in 1 MDCRPS	GCCM - 4
GCCM - 5, 6, 7	GCCM - 5, 6, 7	GEOGRID + NON-WOVEN	GCCM - 5, 6, 7
GCCM - 8	GCCM - 8	GEOCELL + NON-WOVEN	GCCM - 9
CRGR Net	GCCM - 9	-	-
GEOCELL 3D Confinement Protector	-	-	-

Chapter

09

Is there any 'One-size-fits-all' Approach?

The promise of improved efficiency and reduction in costs in infrastructure projects is making many in the infrastructural development circle adopt a generic approach. That is why this approach, although in theory seems practical because of the ability to eliminate variation and set a normal pattern, is often defective and creates much more problems than it solves. **It is very common for many project leaders to be quick in relating and repeating many of the materials and methods they applied in one project to another.**

Common examples include:

- **Shotcrete:** Despite being applied for both slope stabilization and tunnel linings shotcrete appears to have higher inter-changeability. Although it is recognized that even PAM requires adjustments for individual environment and soil conditions, this practice rises and falls with its large-scale application.

- **Stone Pitching:** This method is preferred as it is believed to be easy to use, especially in slope and drainage-related cases. However, it is not applicable in all types of soil and in hydraulic cases as well. Misapplication results in some serious problems such as erosion and structure instability.

Unintended Consequences of Oversimplification

A. Short-Term Savings vs. Long-Term Costs

The single-focus view of affordable costs at the beginning of the implementation of a generalized solution can be rather deceptive.

For example, using shotcrete in various applications without appreciating separate aspects of the environment causes structural failures, like slope protection landslides, which require expensive repair work later.

B. The Maintenance Trap

Generalization can be very costly as it makes maintenance work a lot worse in the future. For instance, stone pitching appears cheap at first, but, more often than not, it disintegrates due to conditions not suited to it.

The result is chronic, costly repairs that were preventable through the use of more appropriate materials for these applications.

Geosynthetic materials and modern geo-solutions may involve slightly higher initial costs but will prove more cost-effective as the days pass by offering durable solutions and greater results.

C. Compromised Performance and Reliability

The repetition of the same solution in different contexts also reduces the general lifespan and efficiency of any project as observed by experts. This means that a material or a method that works in one environment may be significantly less effective under stress, such as stone pitching which yields system degradation and functional failure.

An effective material or method in one case differs from that when tested under different stress levels, for instance, stone pitching in high-velocity water flow areas may result in system degradation and hence functional failures.

The Path Forward: Special Programs

Adapting ideas to the specific requirements of each assignment improves not only efficiency but also can be more beneficial from the economic point of view in the long run.

It is therefore important for leaders in the government and public sectors to think twice when considering the initial appeal of standardisation strategies before considering the long-term outcomes of such proposed solutions.

Key projects and projects that require success demand adaptable and specific solutions when choosing materials and methods of construction that will be sustainable and more successful in infrastructure development.

Most Effective Tailored Modern Geo-Infra Solutions At A Glance

For Slopes	For Drains	For Roads	For Waterproofing
CRGR Net + NON-WOVEN	GCCM + SDA + WHEEPING HOLES	4 in 1 + MURRUM	GCCM + CONCRETE (as a sandwich)
CRGR NET + SDA + NON-WOVEN	3D CONFINEMENT PROTECTOR + NON-WOVEN	6 in 1 + MURRUM	GCCM + DR. FIXIT
GCCM + SDA	GCCM + PCC/RCC (as a sandwich)	3D CONFINEMENT PROTECTOR + PP BIAXIAL SEPARATOR	-
GCCM + SDA + WHEEPING HOLES	GCCM + GABIONS	3D CONFINEMENT PROTECTOR + NON-WOVEN	-
3D CONFINEMENT PROTECTOR + SOIL ANCHORS	3D CONFINEMENT PROTECTOR + PCC/ RCC (as filling material)	PP BIAXIAL SEPARATOR + NON-WOVEN	-
3D CONFINEMENT PROTECTOR + NON-WOVEN	-	-	-
GCCM + GABIONS	-	-	-

Chapter

10

Addressing Situational Challenges with Future-Proof Strategic Advancement

Here's a step-by-step blueprint to successfully address and overcome the situational geo-challenges that are bound to crop up in infrastructure projects.

1. **Proactive Planning and Monitoring**
    - Implementing real-time monitoring systems and predictive maintenance can help identify and address issues before they become critical.
2. **Tailored Solutions**
    - By understanding the specific needs and conditions of each project site, customized solutions can be developed to ensure optimal outcomes.
3. **Balancing Cost with Long-Term Benefits**
    - Investing in advanced technologies and resilient materials can provide significant long-term benefits, including reduced maintenance costs and enhanced project longevity.

4. **Simplifying Regulatory Compliance**

    - Leveraging frameworks like the **IAS 5.0** & next-generation framework - **S M A R T Framework** can streamline compliance processes, ensuring projects meet all necessary standards without unnecessary delays.

By understanding and addressing these practical aspects, infrastructure and geotechnical professionals can enhance their project outcomes, ensuring they are both efficient and resilient in the face of future challenges.

Chapter

11

Modelling Advanced Climate Adaptations:

Weather-Resilient Design Tools

Climate change poses significant challenges to infrastructure projects everywhere. Unpredictable weather patterns, extreme events, and changing environmental conditions require innovative solutions that can adapt and withstand these challenges.

The Impact of Climate Change on Infrastructure

The increasing frequency and intensity of climate-related events such as floods, storms, and heat waves can severely affect infrastructure.

Key impacts include:

1. **Structural Damage:** Extreme weather can cause significant damage to buildings, bridges, and roads, leading to costly repairs and disruptions.
2. **Soil Erosion and Landslides:** Increased rainfall and changing weather patterns can intensify soil erosion and landslides, threatening the stability of slopes and foundations.

3. **Temperature Variations:** Extreme temperatures can affect the durability and performance of construction materials, leading to premature wear and failure.

The Critical Importance of Climate-Resilient Design

Incorporating climate adaptation into infrastructure design is essential for:

1. **Long-Term Sustainability:** Ensuring that infrastructure can withstand future climate conditions reduces the need for frequent repairs and replacements.
2. **Safety and Reliability:** Climate-resilient designs enhance the safety and reliability of infrastructure, protecting lives and investments.
3. **Cost Savings:** By preventing damage and minimizing disruptions, climate-resilient infrastructure leads to significant cost savings over the long term.

Advanced Tools for Weather-Resilient Design

1. **Geosynthetic Solutions:** Geosynthetics are materials used in construction to reinforce soil and improve stability. They play a crucial role in slope protection, erosion control, and drainage systems.
    - **Example:** Reinforced geosynthetic liners can prevent soil erosion on slopes, ensuring long-term stability even during heavy rainfall.
2. **Predictive Modelling Software:** Advanced software tools can simulate the impact of various climate scenarios on

infrastructure projects, allowing engineers to design structures that can withstand extreme conditions.

- **Example:** Software like HEC-RAS (Hydrologic Engineering Centre's River Analysis System) can model the effects of floods on bridge designs, helping engineers create flood-resistant structures.

3. **Green Infrastructure:** Integrating natural elements into infrastructure design can enhance resilience to climate impacts. This includes using vegetation for slope stabilization, constructing wetlands for flood control, and incorporating green roofs to mitigate heat.
   - **Example:** Green roofs can reduce the urban heat island effect and manage stormwater runoff, improving the overall climate resilience of buildings.

Climate-Resilient Roadways: Effective Use-Case Scenario

- Consider a project involving the design of roadways in a region prone to heavy rainfall and flooding.
- By using geosynthetic materials for subgrade stabilization, engineers can ensure that the roads remain stable and functional despite adverse weather conditions.
- Additionally, incorporating green infrastructure such as vegetated swales can help manage stormwater runoff, reducing the risk of flooding.

Integrating Climate Adaptation with the IAS 5.0 Framework

The IAS 5.0 Framework incorporates advanced climate adaptation tools to provide a comprehensive approach to weather-resilient infrastructure.

Here's how it works:

1. **Risk Assessment:** The framework uses predictive modelling to assess the potential impact of climate change on infrastructure projects.
2. **Resilient Design:** It integrates geosynthetic solutions, green infrastructure, and other climate adaptation tools into the design process.
3. **Monitoring and Evaluation:** Continuous monitoring ensures that the infrastructure remains resilient to changing climate conditions, with data-driven insights guiding maintenance and improvements.

Actionable Steps for Implementing Climate-Resilient Design

To effectively incorporate climate adaptation into your infrastructure projects, follow these steps:

- **Conduct Climate Risk Assessments:** Evaluate the potential impacts of climate change on your project sites.
- **Select Appropriate Tools and Materials:** Choose geosynthetics, predictive modelling software, and

green infrastructure solutions that best address your project's needs.

- **Integrate into Design:** Ensure that climate adaptation measures are integrated into the initial design and planning stages.
- **Continuous Monitoring:** Implement monitoring systems to track the performance of climate-resilient features and adjust as needed.
- **Engage Stakeholders:** Collaborate with all stakeholders, including allied government bodies and local communities, to ensure a comprehensive approach to climate resilience.

By adopting advanced climate adaptation tools and integrating them into your infrastructure projects, you can create resilient, sustainable, and future-proof designs that stand up to the challenges posed by climate change.

Chapter

12

Future-Proofing Infrastructure Projects

As infrastructure projects face increasing complexity and unpredictability, future-proofing is the only solution to ensure their long-term resilience and sustainability.

Unimaginable Benefits

1. **Long-Term Viability:** Ensuring that infrastructure remains functional and relevant in the face of changing conditions.
2. **Risk Mitigation:** Anticipating and addressing potential future challenges to minimize their impact.
3. **Cost Efficiency:** Reducing the need for frequent repairs and upgrades by designing infrastructure that can withstand future stresses.
4. **Sustainability:** Promoting environmentally friendly and sustainable practices that protect resources for future generations.

Key Strategies for Future-Proofing

1. **Climate-Resilient Design**
   - Incorporate climate adaptation measures into infrastructure design to withstand extreme weather events and changing environmental conditions.
   - **Example:** Use of flood-resistant materials and elevated structures in flood-prone areas.
2. **Advanced Monitoring Systems**
   - Implement continuous monitoring systems that provide real-time data on infrastructure health and performance.
   - **Example:** DFOS technology for real-time monitoring of bridges and tunnels to detect early signs of stress and damage.
3. **Predictive Maintenance**
   - Utilize predictive maintenance techniques to identify and address potential issues before they lead to significant problems.
   - **Example:** Data analytics and machine learning algorithms to predict maintenance needs based on historical data and current conditions.
4. **Flexible and Modular Design**
   - Design infrastructure with flexibility and modularity in mind, allowing for easy adaptation and expansion as needs change.

- **Example:** Modular construction techniques that enable the addition of new components without major disruptions.

Sustainable Practices

- Integrate sustainable practices into infrastructure projects, such as using renewable energy sources and environmentally friendly materials.
- **Example:** Solar panels for energy generation and recycled materials for construction.

Future-Proofing Urban Transit Systems: A Case Study

The Project: A project aimed at future-proofing an urban transit system in a rapidly growing city.

The Implementation: The project incorporates several strategies to ensure long-term resilience and sustainability:

1. **Climate-Resilient Infrastructure:** Elevated rail tracks and flood-resistant stations are designed to withstand extreme weather events.
2. **Advanced Monitoring:** DFOS technology is used to continuously monitor the condition of tracks and stations, providing real-time data on structural health.
3. **Predictive Maintenance:** Data analytics tools predict maintenance needs, ensuring timely interventions and minimizing disruptions.

4. **Modular Design:** The transit system is designed with modular components that can be easily expanded as the city's population grows.
5. **Sustainable Energy:** Solar panels are installed at stations to generate renewable energy, reducing the system's carbon footprint.

By integrating these future-proofing strategies, the urban transit system is equipped to handle future challenges and continue to serve the city's growing population effectively.

Integrating Future-Proofing with the S M A R T Framework

The S M A R T Framework supports future-proofing by providing a comprehensive approach to managing infrastructure projects:

1. **Real-Time Insights:** Continuous monitoring and data integration provide real-time insights into infrastructure health and performance.
2. **Predictive Analytics:** Advanced analytics tools predict potential future challenges and recommend preventive measures.
3. **Sustainable Practices:** The framework promotes the use of sustainable materials and practices in infrastructure design and construction.

Actionable Steps for Future-Proofing Infrastructure Projects

To effectively future-proof your infrastructure projects, consider the following steps:

- **Assess Future Risks:** Identify potential future challenges, such as climate change, population growth, and technological advancements.
- **Incorporate Resilient Design:** Integrate climate-resilient and flexible design elements into your projects.
- **Implement Advanced Monitoring:** Use continuous monitoring systems to provide real-time data on infrastructure health.
- **Utilize Predictive Maintenance:** Apply predictive maintenance techniques to anticipate and address potential issues.
- **Adopt Sustainable Practices:** Use renewable energy sources and environmentally friendly materials to promote sustainability.

By adopting these strategies and integrating them into your project management processes, you can ensure that your infrastructure projects are resilient, sustainable, and prepared for future challenges.

Chapter

13

Two Choices: Implement Solo or Seek Guidance

As we wrap up our journey through the world of advanced geotechnical solutions and infrastructure innovation, let's revisit the essentials simply and clearly.

Think of this recap as your quick guide to confidently enhancing your infrastructure projects with the latest technologies and strategies.

- We started with the need for transformation in the ever-rising infrastructure and geo landscape due to modern-day challenges coupled with old-age structural deficits.
- This urgency to resolve infra and geo challenges led to the advent of an innovative infra and geo challenges resolution, wherein lies my core expertise.
- My journey resulted in the development of the IAS 5.0 Framework and SMART Framework.
- These contributions, milestones, and industry accolades have set new standards, with numerous testimonials reflecting the impact of these new-age solutions on

geotechnical engineering and infrastructure innovation.

- This expertise bridges traditional methods with modern technologies, offering practical solutions to transform infrastructure projects into milestones.
- Then I shared a comprehensive understanding of the fresh perspective of solving infra-geo challenges and discovering advanced geotechnical practices and their ground-breaking benefits unfold with selected examples.
- Before raising the curtain on the solutions, I shared a quick glimpse of market realities, often coloured by myths and misconceptions, which helps to explore the core of the challenges faced in the geotechnical sector.
- Proactive planning and tailored solutions appear as the two essentials for overcoming situational crises and achieving project success.
- Tailored solutions highlight the steps for developing and implementing custom geotechnical solutions, emphasizing the importance of site-specific approaches and providing relevant case studies.
- We also looked closely at strategies and tools to streamline the compliance process, integrating them with the IAS 5.0 Framework to ensure the seamless execution of projects.
- Continuous health monitoring and predictive maintenance are key to infrastructure longevity. We meet advanced technologies and techniques, with case

studies on their effective implementation in tunnel management.

- Real-time monitoring is vital for infrastructure health. DFOS technology provides continuous data, enabling early detection of issues.
- Climate change impacts infrastructure projects significantly. Here, we meet tools and technologies for climate-resilient design, ensuring long-term viability and sustainability, with a case study on resilient roadways demonstrating practical applications.
- Future-proofing ensures long-term resilience and sustainability. It discusses strategies for anticipating and mitigating future risks, integrating climate-resilient design and sustainable practices.

Two Choices: Implement Independently or Seek Expert Guidance

As we conclude our journey through advanced geotechnical solutions, you come to stand at a crossroads.

Choice One

Implement the knowledge independently, using this guide as a reference, and adopt the best measures to upkeep your geo/infra projects. Choose the practical path that best suits your needs to achieve infrastructure excellence.

Stay connected for more insights and updates.

Choice Two

If you want your projects to proceed in an absolutely smooth, speedy, and seamless manner with tailored strategies under expert guidance.

Book your Discovery Call at........

Scan QR to fill a form and also scan to WhatsApp or email **sanbros@ssplngp.com**

Together, we can build a future of resilient, efficient, and exemplary infrastructure projects.

Irrespective of the choice you make, I would love to have your feedback. Write to me at-

sanbros@ssplngp.com

Also, if you are interested in learning about new technologies, innovative ways to address geo/infra challenges, or actionable insights to enhance the efficiency of your geo/infra projects then you can always connect with me on

LinkedIn.

I once again, express my wishes for your dedication to enhancing the infrastructure landscape and fortifying the geo segment. I assure you that together, we can build a future that is both functional and exemplary.

For being such a great reader and being committed to learning new ways of ensuring your infra projects are super successful, I have a very special gift for you —

Two Bonus Chapters on Strategic Monitoring and Cutting-Edge

Safety Enhancements

So, read on for extra actionable info to make your projects leap to the highest levels of success and efficiency.

Bonus Chapter 1

Strategic Monitoring: Real-Time Infrastructure Insights

In the field of infrastructure development and sustenance, timely and accurate information is critical for sustainability and optimal performance. The foundation of effective project management lies in the ability to monitor and assess the state of infrastructure in real-time, every time.

Why Real-Time Monitoring?

Real-time monitoring allows project heads to gain a comprehensive view of their infrastructure's health and performance. By continuously tracking key metrics and identifying potential issues early, real-time monitoring helps in:

1. **Proactive Maintenance:** Early detection of issues enables timely interventions, preventing minor problems from escalating into major failures.
2. **Safety Assurance:** Continuous monitoring ensures that any structural weaknesses or risks are identified and addressed promptly, enhancing overall safety.
3. **Cost Efficiency:** By reducing the need for extensive repairs and prolonging the lifespan of infrastructure, real-time monitoring leads to significant cost savings.

Advanced Monitoring Technologies

One of the most ground-breaking technologies in this field is Distributed Fiber Optic Sensing (DFOS).

DFOS utilizes fibre optic cables as continuous sensors to monitor various parameters such as temperature, strain, and vibrations.

Here's how DFOS contributes to real-time infrastructure insights:

1. **Comprehensive Data Collection:** DFOS provides extensive coverage and precise data collection, enabling a detailed understanding of infrastructure conditions.
2. **High Sensitivity:** The technology detects even the slightest changes, ensuring early identification of potential issues.
3. **Durability and Reliability:** Fiber optic sensors are robust and can operate in harsh environments, making them ideal for infrastructure monitoring.

DFOS in Action: Use-Case Scenario

Consider the application of DFOS in monitoring railway tunnels. The continuous sensing capabilities of DFOS enable real-time detection of stress points, temperature fluctuations, and potential structural weaknesses. By analysing this data, railway authorities can implement targeted maintenance, ensuring the safety and reliability of the tunnels.

Integrating Real-Time Insights with IAS 5.0 Framework

The IAS 5.0 Framework leverages advanced monitoring technologies like DFOS to provide a unified view of infrastructure health. Here's how it works:

1. **Data Integration:** The framework integrates data from various sources, including DFOS sensors, to offer a holistic view of infrastructure conditions.
2. **Real-Time Dashboards:** Custom dashboards display real-time data, making it easy to spot issues and trends.
3. **Predictive Analytics:** The framework uses advanced analytics to predict potential failures and recommend preventive measures.

Actionable Steps for Implementing Real-Time Monitoring

To harness the benefits of real-time monitoring, consider the following steps:

- **Assess Your Needs:** Identify the key parameters that need monitoring based on the specific requirements of your project.
- **Choose the Right Technology:** Select monitoring technologies that align with your project's needs. DFOS is an excellent choice for comprehensive, real-time data collection.

- **Integrate with Existing Systems:** Ensure that the monitoring system integrates seamlessly with your existing project management tools.
- **Train Your Team:** Provide training to your team on how to interpret the data and use it for proactive decision-making.
- **Regular Reviews:** Conduct regular reviews of the monitoring data to identify trends and adjust your maintenance strategies accordingly.

By implementing strategic monitoring and leveraging real-time insights, you can significantly enhance the efficiency, safety, and longevity of your infrastructure projects.

Bonus Chapter 2

Advanced Resilient Technologies: Cutting-Edge Safety Enhancements

In the fast-paced world of infrastructure development, ensuring the safety and resilience of projects is paramount. Advanced technologies play a crucial role in enhancing safety, reducing risks, and ensuring long-term durability.

Here our focus is on cutting-edge safety enhancements that can revolutionize infrastructure projects, with a particular emphasis on Distributed Fiber Optic Sensing (DFOS) and QMAX technologies.

The Importance of Advanced Safety Technologies

Advanced safety technologies are essential for:

1. **Risk Mitigation:** Identifying and addressing potential hazards before they lead to significant problems.
2. **Structural Integrity:** Ensuring that infrastructure can withstand various stresses and remain functional over time.
3. **Operational Efficiency:** Reducing downtime and maintenance costs by proactively managing safety concerns.

Distributed Fiber Optic Sensing (DFOS)

DFOS is a ground-breaking technology that uses fibre optic cables as continuous sensors to monitor various parameters such as strain, temperature, and vibrations.

Here's how DFOS enhances infrastructure safety:

1. **Comprehensive Monitoring:** DFOS provides continuous, real-time data across extensive areas, offering a detailed understanding of infrastructure conditions.
2. **High Sensitivity:** The technology detects minute changes, enabling early identification of potential issues.
3. **Durability:** Fiber optic sensors are robust and can operate in challenging environments, making them ideal for infrastructure monitoring.

DFOS in Bridge Monitoring: Use-Case Scenario

Consider the application of DFOS in monitoring a bridge. The continuous sensing capabilities of DFOS allow for real-time detection of stress points and temperature fluctuations, ensuring that any potential structural weaknesses are identified and addressed promptly. This proactive approach enhances the safety and longevity of the bridge.

QMAX Technology

QMAX is another innovative technology that significantly contributes to infrastructure safety and efficiency. It is designed to provide precise detection and resolution for electronic components used in various infrastructure applications.

1. **Precision Detection:** QMAX technology offers highly accurate detection of faults and irregularities in electronic systems.
2. **Efficient Resolution:** It enables quick identification and resolution of issues, minimizing downtime and operational disruptions.
3. **Versatility:** QMAX can be applied across different types of infrastructure, from transportation systems to power grids.

QMAX in Railway Systems: Use-Case Scenario

In the context of railway systems, QMAX technology can be used to monitor and maintain electronic components in locomotives and signalling systems. By ensuring the precise functioning of these components, QMAX enhances the safety and reliability of railway operations, reducing the risk of accidents and service interruptions.

Integrating Advanced Technologies with the SMART Framework

The **SMART Framework** leverages both DFOS and QMAX technologies to provide a comprehensive safety solution for infrastructure projects. Here's how it integrates these technologies:

1. **Data Collection:** The framework uses DFOS for real-time monitoring and data collection, providing continuous insights into infrastructure conditions.
2. **Fault Detection:** QMAX technology is employed for precise detection and resolution of electronic system faults, ensuring optimal performance.
3. **Holistic Safety Management:** By combining these technologies, the IAS 5.0 Framework offers a holistic approach to managing infrastructure safety, from structural integrity to electronic system reliability.

Actionable Steps for Implementing Advanced Safety Technologies

To effectively integrate advanced safety technologies into your infrastructure projects, follow these steps:

1. **Assess Safety Needs:** Identify the key safety concerns for your project and determine where advanced technologies can provide the most benefit.

2. **Select Appropriate Technologies:** Choose technologies like DFOS and QMAX that align with your project's specific safety requirements.
3. **Integrate into Project Planning:** Ensure that these technologies are integrated into the initial design and planning stages of your project.
4. **Continuous Monitoring:** Implement continuous monitoring systems to track the performance and safety of your infrastructure.
5. **Training and Maintenance:** Provide training for your team on how to use and maintain these technologies effectively.

By adopting advanced safety technologies like DFOS and QMAX, you can significantly enhance the safety, efficiency, and resilience of your infrastructure projects.